Editor
Eric Migliaccio

Editor in Chief
Karen J. Goldfluss, M.S. Ed.

Creative Director
Sarah M. Smith

Cover Artist
Barb Lorseyedi

Art Coordinator
Renée Mc Elwee

Illustrator
Kelly McMahon

Imaging
James Edward Grace

Publisher
Mary D. Smith, M.S. Ed.

Author
Heather Wolpert-Gawron

For correlations to Common Core State Standards, see page 8 of this book or visit *http://www.teachercreated.com/standards/*.

Teacher Created Resources
6421 Industry Way
Westminster, CA 92683
www.teachercreated.com

ISBN: 978-1-4206-3822-6

Made in U.S.A.

Table of Contents

Introduction

Reading and comprehending nonfiction or informational text is a challenge. Not everyone can do it well, and it needs to be specifically taught. Students who are great at reading narratives like *Lord of the Rings* or *The Princess Diaries* may still quiver at the possibility of having to understand instructions on uploading an assignment to DropBox. Students who love reading historical fiction may be fearful of reading history. Students who, with flashlight in hand, hide beneath their sheets reading the end of a science-fiction book may glaze over at the sight of an actual factual science article.

Nevertheless, informational text is all around us, and reading it well just takes working out a certain muscle — an informational-text muscle, if you will.

This book is meant to be an informational-muscle gym. Each activity is meant to build in complexity, and each activity is meant to push students in both their reading and their ability to display what they understand about what they read.

In addition to a practice passage, there are 18 reading selections contained in this book. The selections are separated into units, based on their subject matter. As a result, no matter the content area you teach, you will find applicable selections here on which your students can practice.

It doesn't matter what state you teach in, what grade level you teach, or what subject you teach; this book will aid students in understanding more deeply the difficult task of reading informational and nonfiction texts.

Reading Comprehension and the Common Core

The Common Core Standards are here, and with them come a different way to think about reading comprehension. In the past, reading informational text had been compartmentalized, each piece an isolated activity. The Common Core way of thinking is slightly different.

The goal is for students to read different genres and selections of text, pull them together in their heads, and be able to derive a theme or topic that may be shared by them all. In other words, a student may be given three different texts from three different points of view or three different genre standpoints and then have to think about their own thoughts on the subject.

Perhaps a student looks at the following:

1. Instructions on downloading an image from a digital camera
2. A biography about a famous photographer
3. A Google search history on the invention of the camera from the past to the present

Then, from those pieces, the student must pull a common theme or opinion on the topic.

Introduction *(cont.)*

Reading Comprehension and the Common Core *(cont.)*

But to be able to synthesize text (put the thoughts together), a student must first be able to read individual texts and analyze them (pull them apart). That's where this series of books comes in.

Nonfiction Reading Comprehension for the Common Core helps students to hone in on a specific piece of text, identify what's the most important concept in that piece, and answer questions about that specific selection. This will train your students for the bigger challenge that will come later in their schooling: viewing multiple texts and shaking out the meaning of them all.

If you are a public-school teacher, you may be in a state that has adopted the Common Core Standards. Use the selections in this book as individual reading-comprehension activities or pair them with similarly themed selections from other genres to give students a sense of how they will have to pull understanding from the informational, text-heavy world around us.

Copy the individual worksheets as is; or, if you are looking for a more Common Core-aligned format, mimic the Common Core multiple-choice assessments that are coming our way by entering the questions into websites that can help create computer adaptive tests (CATs).

CATs are assessments that allow a student to answer a question, which, depending on whether they answered it correctly or not, leads them to the next question that may be more geared to his or her level. In other words, each student will be taking a differentiated assessment that will end up indicating if a student is capable of answering "Novice" questions up to "Expert" questions.

There are many websites out there that can help you develop assessments to mimic those planned. Create the quiz and embed it into your class webpage or document:

Here are just a couple:

- *http://www.gotoquiz.com/create.html*
- *http://www.quibblo.com/*

Use the selections from this book, and then enter the corresponding questions into the quiz generators. We have identified questions that are higher or lower in level by assigning them a "weight" (from single-weight up through triple-weight). This weight system provides a glimpse of how hard a student should work in order to answer the question correctly. (For more information, read "Leveled Questions" on page 5.)

Regardless of how you choose to use this book, introducing students to the informational world at large is an important way to help them build skills that they will use throughout their schooling and beyond.

Leveled Questions

As you go through this book, you will notice that each question that students will be answering is labeled with icons that look like weights. These icons represent different levels of difficulty. The levels are based on Costa's Levels of Questioning.

The questions in this book are divided into three levels:

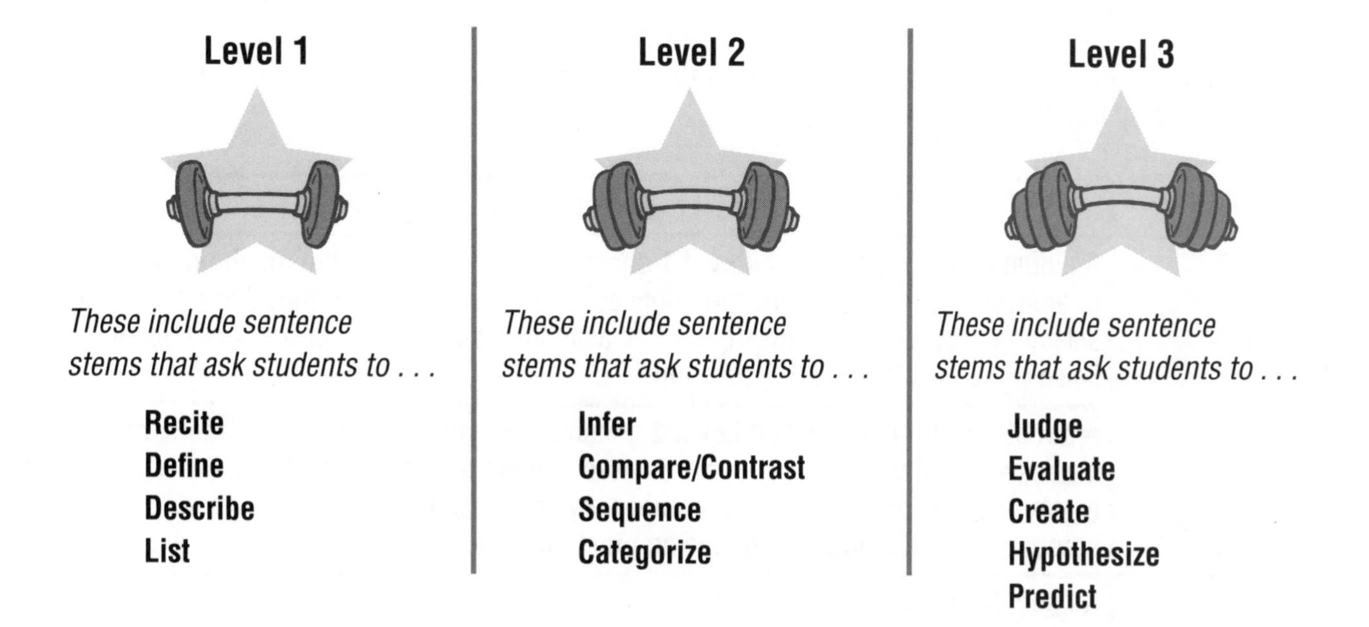

The icons are a visual way to make these levels clear to students. That is important because students need to be able to recognize that some questions may require more effort and thought to answer.

Now, most of the multiple-choice questions in this book happen to fall into the Level 1 and Level 2 categories. That is pretty standard for multiple-choice questions. After all, how can asking to create something be defined by an A, B, C, or D answer? However, we may have found a way around that.

At the end of each worksheet is a place for students to develop their own questions about the material they have just read. This brings in a deeper-thinking opportunity. Having your students ask higher-level questions is a great way for assessing their comprehension of what they have read. The deeper the student's question, the deeper his or her understanding of the material.

A student handout called "The Questioning Rubric" is provided on page 6. It serves two purposes:

- It gives your students concrete examples of the elements that make up the different levels of questions.
- It gives you, the teacher, a way to determine whether a student-generated question is a low- or high-level inquiry.

The goal of a student is to ask more challenging questions of oneself. The goal of the teacher is to be able to track better the level of production for each student. This book helps do both.

Introduction *(cont.)*

The Questioning Rubric

Answering questions is one way of proving you understand a reading selection. However, creating your very own questions about the selection might be an even better way. Developing thoughtful, high-level questions can really display your understanding of what you have read, and it also makes other students think about the reading passage in a unique way.

So what types of questions can you ask? There are three levels of questions, and for each one there is a different amount of work your brain must do to answer the question. We've chosen to use a symbol of a weight in order to represent this amount. Consult this chart when thinking about what defines a great question as compared to a so-so one.

Icon	Description
	A single weight represents a **Level 1** question that doesn't require much brainpower to answer correctly. The question only asks readers to tell what they know about the selection. For example, any inquiry that asks for a simple "Yes or No" or "True or False" response is a Level 1 question.
	A double weight represents a **Level 2** question that requires you to use a little more brain sweat. (Ewww!) This question asks readers to think a little beyond the passage. It may require some analysis, inference, or interpretation. Questions involving comparing/contrasting or sequencing often fall here.
	A **Level 3** question really makes you work for its answer. These questions allow you to show off your knowledge of a topic by asking you to create, wonder, judge, evaluate, and/or apply what you know to what you think. These types of questions are much more open-ended than Level 1 or Level 2 questions.

Don't be scared to sweat a little in answering or developing Level 3 questions. Working out your brain in this way will help prepare you for some heavy lifting later on in life. So as you progress through this book, use this rubric as a resource to make sure your questions are as high-level as possible.

Need help getting started? The following sentence stems will give you ideas about how to create questions for each level.

Level 1

- Write the definition of…
- Describe how _____ is…
- List the details that go into…

Level 2

- What can you infer from _____?
- Compare _____ with _____.
- Contrast _____ with _____.
- Write the steps in sequence from _____.
- Place _____ in the right category.

Level 3

- How would you judge the _____?
- How would you evaluate the _____?
- How can you create a _____?
- Hypothesize what would happen if _____.
- What do you predict will happen in _____?

Introduction *(cont.)*

Achievement Graph

As you correct your responses in this book, track how well you improve. Calculate how many answers you got right after each worksheet and mark your progress here based on the number of weights each question was worth. For instance, if you get the first problem correct and it is worth two weights, then write "2" in the first column. Do this for each column and add up your total at the end.

Reading Passage	1	2	3	4	Total
The Star of the Sea					
Matter Matters					
The Fish with the Big Mouth					
Not a Planet Now					
A Home for *Endeavour*					
The Colors a Shrimp Sees					
Castles					
How They Got Their Name					
Big Dinosaur, Small Brain					
The History of the Fire Truck					
A Magical Way to Travel					
The Man Who Did So Much					
The "Fab Four" Friends					
The Flying Squirrel					
Some More, Please!					
Taking Care of a Dog					
How to Create a Poll					
What Is a Palindrome?					
Making Paper Fly					

Common Core State Standards

The lessons and activities included in *Nonfiction Reading Comprehension for the Common Core, Grade 2* meet the following Common Core State Standards. (©Copyright 2010. National Governors Association Center for Best Practices and Council of Chief State School Officers. All right reserved.) For more information about the Common Core State Standards, go to *http://www.corestandards.org/* or visit *http://www.teachercreated.com/standards/*.

Informational Text Standards	
Key Ideas and Details	**Pages**
CCSS.ELA.RI.2.1. Ask and answer such questions as *who, what, where, when, why,* and *how* to demonstrate understanding of key details in a text.	10-47
Craft and Structure	**Pages**
CCSS.ELA.RI.2.4. Determine the meaning of words and phrases in a text relevant to a *grade 2 topic or subject area.*	10-47
Range of Reading and Level of Text Complexity	**Pages**
CCSS.ELA.RI.2.10. By the end of year, read and comprehend informational texts in the grades 2–3 text complexity band proficiently, with scaffolding as needed at the high end of the range.	10-47
Foundational Skills Standards	
Phonics and Word Recognition	**Pages**
CCSS.ELA.RF.2.3. Know and apply grade-level phonics and word analysis skills in decoding words.	10-47
Fluency	**Pages**
CCSS.ELA.RF.2.4. Read with sufficient accuracy and fluency to support comprehension.	10-47
Language Standards	
Conventions of Standard English	**Pages**
CCSS.ELA.L.2.1. Demonstrate command of the conventions of standard English grammar and usage when writing or speaking.	11-47
CCSS.ELA.L.2.2. Demonstrate command of the conventions of standard English capitalization, punctuation, and spelling when writing.	11-47
Knowledge of Language	**Pages**
CCSS.ELA.L.2.3. Use knowledge of language and its conventions when writing, speaking, reading, or listening.	10-47
Vocabulary Acquisition and Use	**Pages**
CCSS.ELA.L.2.4. Determine or clarify the meaning of unknown and multiple-meaning words and phrases based on *grade 2 reading and content,* choosing flexibly from an array of strategies.	10-47
Writing Standards	
Research to Build and Present Knowledge	**Pages**
CCSS.ELA.W.2.8. Recall information from experiences or gather information from provided sources to answer a question.	10-47

Multiple-Choice Test-Taking Tips

Some multiple-choice questions are straightforward and easy. "I know the answer!" your brain yells right away. Some questions, however, stump even the most prepared student. In cases like that, you have to make an educated guess. An educated guess is a guess that uses what you know to help guide your attempt. You don't put your hand over your eyes and pick a random letter! You select it because you've thought about the format of the question, the word choice, the other possible answers, and the language of what's being asked. By making an educated guess, you're increasing your chances of guessing correctly. Whenever you are taking a multiple-choice assessment, you should remember to follow the rules below:

1. Read the directions. It's crucial. You may assume you know what is being asked, but sometimes directions can be tricky when you least expect them to be.
2. Read the questions before you read the passage. Doing this allows you to read the text through a more educated and focused lens. For example, if you know that you will be asked to identify the main idea, you can be on the lookout for that ahead of time.
3. Don't skip a question. Instead, try to make an educated guess. That starts with crossing off the ones you definitely know are not the correct answer. For instance, if you have four possible answers (A, B, C, D) and you can cross off two of them immediately, you've doubled your chances of guessing correctly. If you don't cross off any obvious ones, you would only have a 25% chance of guessing right. However, if you cross off two, you now have a 50% chance!
4. Read carefully for words like *always*, *never*, *not*, *except*, and *every*. Words like these are there to make you stumble. They make the question very specific. Sometimes an answer can be right some of the time, but if a word like *always* or *every* is in the question, the answer must be right *all of the time.*
5. After reading a question, try to come up with the answer first in your head before looking at the possible answers. That way, you will be less likely to bubble or click something you aren't sure about.
6. In questions with an "All of the Above" answer, think of it this way: if you can identify at least two that are correct, then "All of the Above" is probably the correct answer.
7. In questions with a "None of the Above" answer, think of it this way: if you can identify at least two that are *not* correct, then "None of the Above" is probably the correct answer.
8. Don't keep changing your answer. Unless you are sure you made a mistake, usually the first answer you chose is the right one.

Practice Passage

The Star of the Sea

The starfish is one of the most interesting animals in the ocean. Did you know that scientists do not call this creature by the name *starfish*? They call it a sea star. That is because the "starfish" is not a fish at all.

There are many reasons why the sea star is so interesting. Here are six of those reasons:

1. There are about 200 kinds of sea stars.
2. They live in saltwater. They live all over the world.
3. Most have five legs, but some have more. Some have as many as 40 legs.
4. If a sea star loses a leg, it can grow it back.
5. A whole new sea star can grow from a leg that has broken off.
6. A sea star's stomach can come out of its body to eat food! Then the stomach returns to its body.

Sea stars come in all sizes. They also come in many bright colors. That is one reason why people put them in their aquariums at home. Sea stars add a lot of color.

Name: ______________________ Practice Passage

Answer the following questions about the story "The Star of the Sea." The weights show you how hard you will need to work to find each answer.

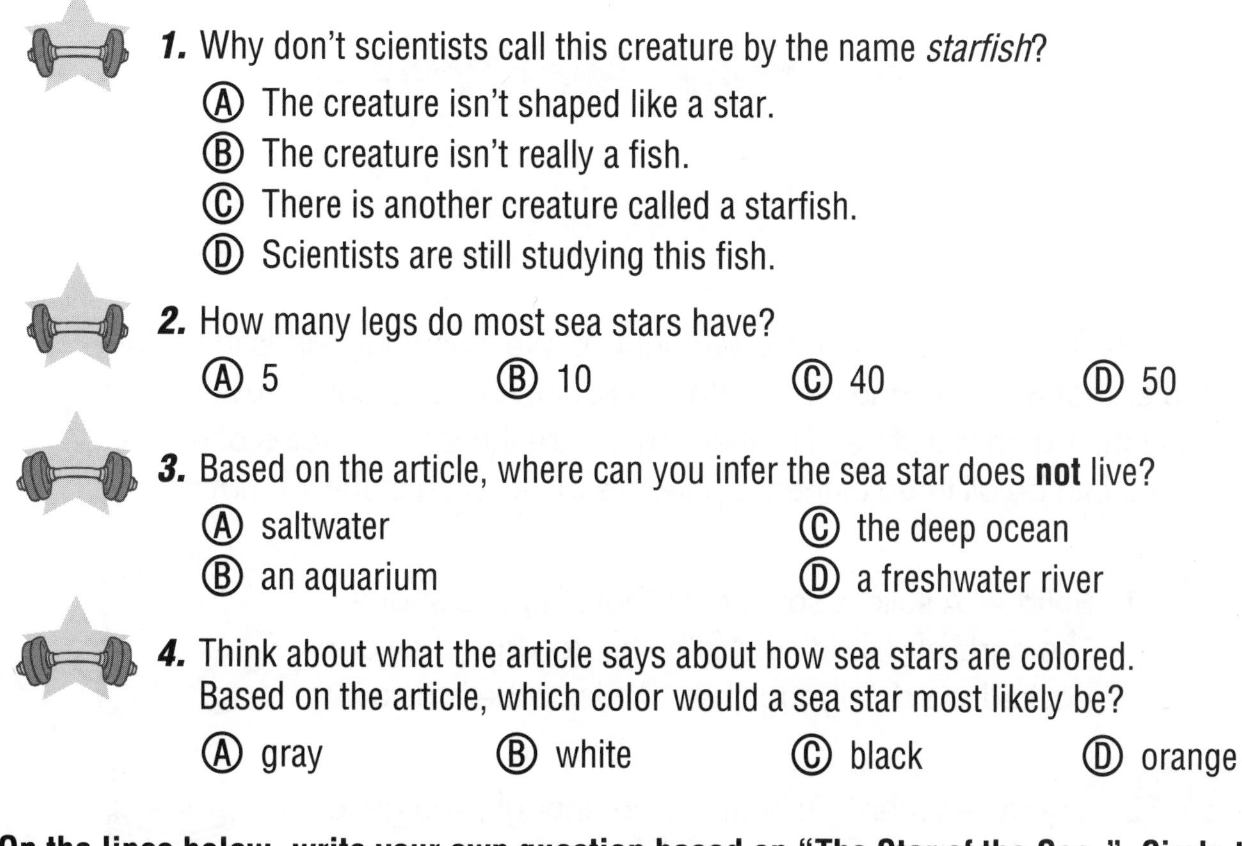

1. Why don't scientists call this creature by the name *starfish*?

Ⓐ The creature isn't shaped like a star.

Ⓑ The creature isn't really a fish.

Ⓒ There is another creature called a starfish.

Ⓓ Scientists are still studying this fish.

2. How many legs do most sea stars have?

Ⓐ 5 Ⓑ 10 Ⓒ 40 Ⓓ 50

3. Based on the article, where can you infer the sea star does **not** live?

Ⓐ saltwater

Ⓑ an aquarium

Ⓒ the deep ocean

Ⓓ a freshwater river

4. Think about what the article says about how sea stars are colored. Based on the article, which color would a sea star most likely be?

Ⓐ gray Ⓑ white Ⓒ black Ⓓ orange

On the lines below, write your own question based on "The Star of the Sea." Circle the correct picture on the left to show the level of the question you wrote.

____

____

____

____

On a separate piece of paper . . .

- Write a sentence that includes the word *interesting*.
- Which fact about the sea star do you find the most interesting? Why?

Science Passage #1

Matter Matters

We use water all the time. We drink it. We wash our hands in it. The water that we drink and wash with is a liquid. Water is not always a liquid, though. Liquid is a state of matter. There are three main states of matter. Water can be all three of them. Here are those three states of matter:

1. **Solid** — A solid is something that keeps its shape. The parts of a solid cannot be broken up. They are packed too closely together. An ice cube is a solid.

2. **Liquid** — When you heat a solid enough, you get a liquid. A liquid changes its shape. It can become the shape of its *container.* Water is a liquid. When you put it into a cup, it fills in the shape of the cup.

3. **Gas** — Heated liquid can become a gas. A gas is hard to see. The air we breathe is a gas. Steam is also a gas. You get steam when you heat water.

Look at the steam from your bath. Think about where the water came from. Look at the fog through the trees. Think about the different states of matter. Your bath water may have once been a piece of ice from a very cold part of the world. The fog you see may have come from the ocean. Neat, huh?

Answer the following questions about the story "Matter Matters." The weights show you how hard you will need to work to find each answer.

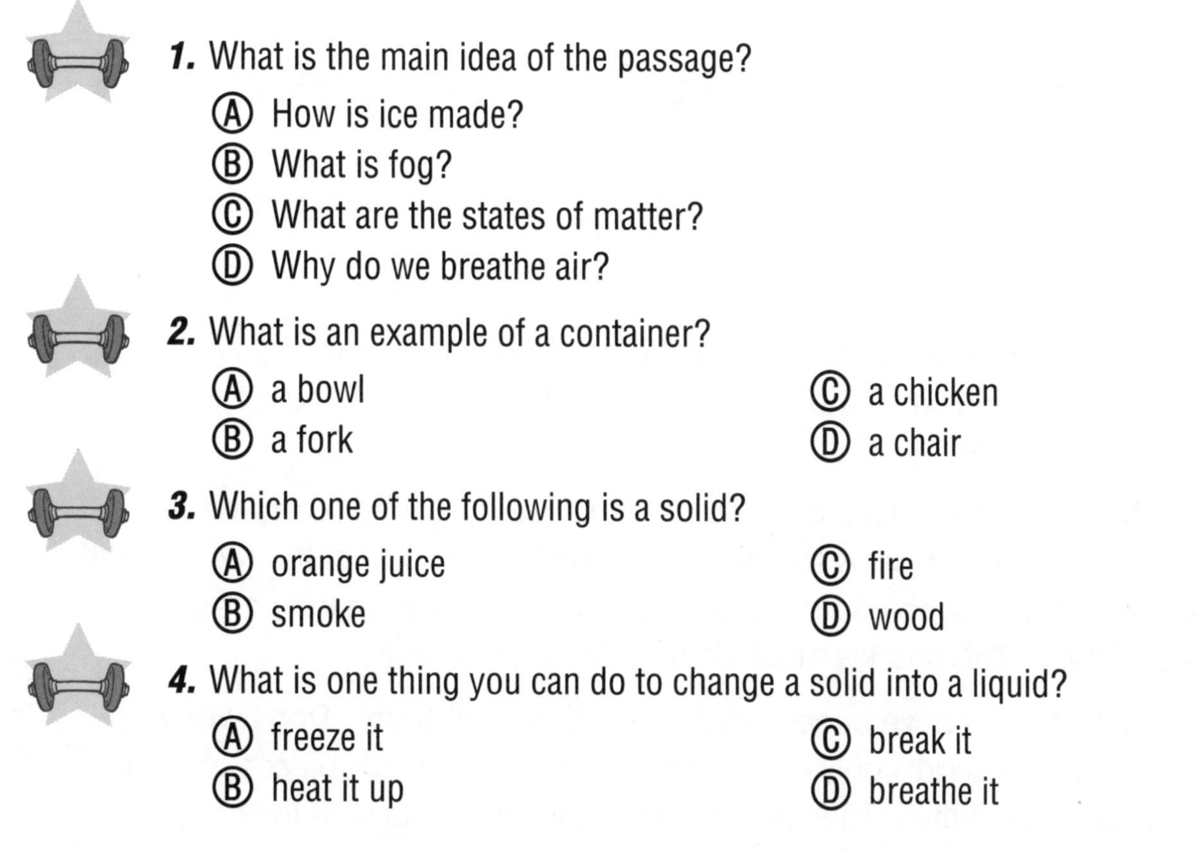

1. What is the main idea of the passage?

Ⓐ How is ice made?
Ⓑ What is fog?
Ⓒ What are the states of matter?
Ⓓ Why do we breathe air?

2. What is an example of a container?

Ⓐ a bowl
Ⓑ a fork
Ⓒ a chicken
Ⓓ a chair

3. Which one of the following is a solid?

Ⓐ orange juice
Ⓑ smoke
Ⓒ fire
Ⓓ wood

4. What is one thing you can do to change a solid into a liquid?

Ⓐ freeze it
Ⓑ heat it up
Ⓒ break it
Ⓓ breathe it

On the lines below, write your own question based on "Matter Matters." Circle the correct picture on the left to show the level of the question you wrote.

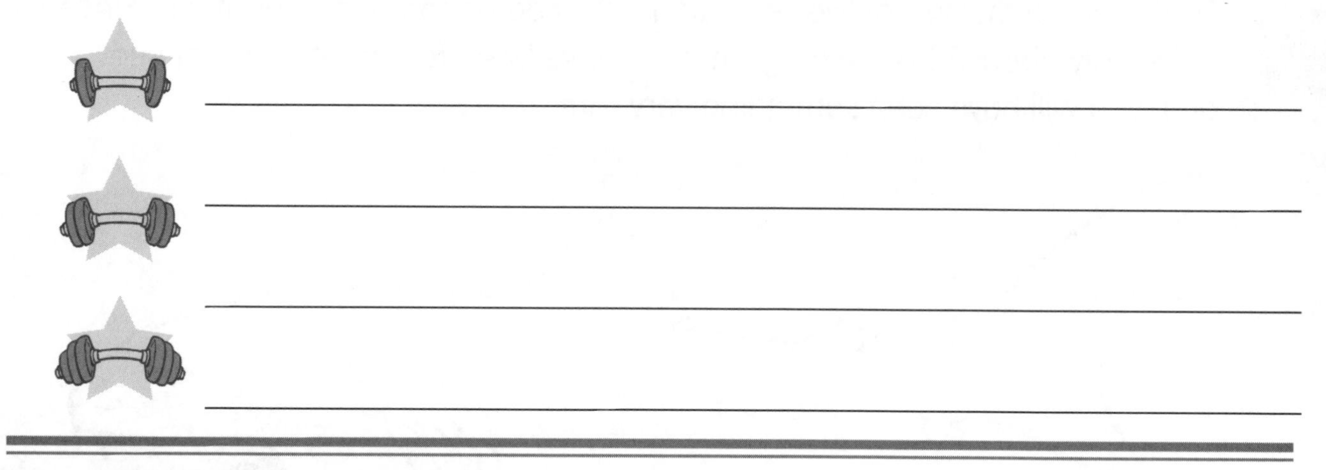

On a separate piece of paper . . .

- Write a sentence that includes the word *steam.*
- Think about the clouds. Do you think they are a solid, a liquid, or a gas? Explain your answer.

Science Passage #2

The Fish with the Big Mouth

Some sharks are scary and big. Some sharks are small and won't hurt you. There is one shark that is bigger than all of them. It is called the megamouth shark.

Megamouth sharks are very *rare*. We have not found many in the ocean. Can you guess by its name what the biggest part of the Megamouth may be? You probably said "its mouth." You are right! In fact, *mega*- means "big." This shark's mouth is huge and full of teeth.

These sharks have huge bodies, too. They look scary. Don't worry, though. These sharks only eat food like jellyfish and small pieces of food that float in the water. They get their food by swimming with their big mouths wide open. The food just swims or floats right in!

The first megamouth was discovered in 1976. It was about 15 feet long. That is about the size of five 1st graders stacked on top of one another! Since 1976, only about 50 more megamouths have been found. If you ever see one, you will have seen something very rare.

Answer the following questions about the story "The Fish with the Big Mouth." The weights show you how hard you will need to work to find each answer.

1. If you use *mega-* in front of the word *phone*, you get *megaphone*. Based on what *mega* means, a *megaphone* would most likely be

Ⓐ quiet. Ⓑ loud. Ⓒ funny. Ⓓ strange.

2. What is one thing megamouth sharks eat?

Ⓐ pizza
Ⓑ jellyfish
Ⓒ whales
Ⓓ other sharks

3. How does a megamouth shark catch its food?

Ⓐ It goes fishing with a pole.
Ⓑ It scoops it up with its fins.
Ⓒ It catches it in a net.
Ⓓ It swims with its mouth open.

4. What does the word *rare* mean?

Ⓐ There are many of them.
Ⓑ They are interesting.
Ⓒ They are sad.
Ⓓ There are not a lot of them.

On the lines below, write your own question based on "The Fish with the Big Mouth." Circle the correct picture on the left to show the level of the question you wrote.

____

____

____

____

On a separate piece of paper . . .

- Write a sentence that includes the word *rare*.
- Megamouth sharks are named after their big mouths. If you could name another animal after something it has, which animal would you choose? What new name would you give for that animal?

Science Passage #3

Not a Planet Now

Have you heard of a place called Pluto? It was once considered a planet. In 1930, a large object was seen in space. It was very far from Earth. It was made of rock and ice. It was smaller than Earth's moon. A vote was taken to name it. The name "Pluto" was chosen. We had eight planets in our solar system. It was decided that Pluto was the ninth.

However, Pluto is not called a planet now. Poor little planet! In 2006, scientists decided that Pluto was not a planet after all. They said that it wasn't big enough. They also said that its *gravity* wasn't strong enough. Gravity is the force that pulls things down to the ground. Do you jump up sometimes? What always happens when you jump up? Don't you always come back down? Gravity does this. It is the force that pulls you back to the ground.

Pluto's gravity is not as strong as Earth's. Pluto also is not as big as Earth. It is still a big rock, though. We still learn about this giant rock that isn't quite big enough to be a planet.

Name: ______________________________

Answer the following questions about the story "Not a Planet Now." The weights show you how hard you will need to work to find each answer.

1. What is *gravity*?

Ⓐ A force that pushes you away from the ground
Ⓑ A force that pushes you across the ground
Ⓒ A force that pulls you down to the ground
Ⓓ A force that bounces you around the clouds

2. How do you think the author feels about Pluto?

Ⓐ The author hates the planet.
Ⓑ The author feels sorry for the planet.
Ⓒ The author likes stars.
Ⓓ The author does not like our moon.

3. In what year was Pluto found?

Ⓐ 2006 Ⓑ 1930 Ⓒ 1500 Ⓓ 2012

4. Pluto is ____________ than Earth.

Ⓐ bigger Ⓑ funnier Ⓒ stronger Ⓓ smaller

On the lines below, write your own question based on "Not a Planet Now." Circle the correct picture on the left to show the level of the question you wrote.

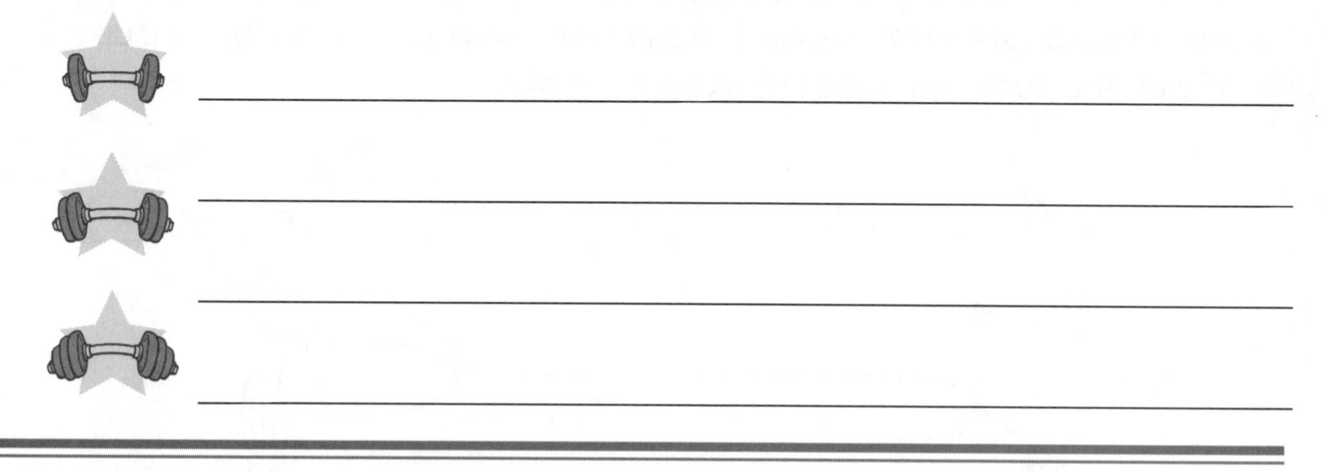

On a separate piece of paper . . .

- Write a sentence that includes the word *gravity*.
- Pluto was named by a little girl. She named it after a Roman god. Pluto is a cold, dark planet. What would you name a cold, dark planet? Why would you name it that?

Science Passage #4

A Home for *Endeavour*

It did not used to be easy to see a space shuttle up close. Not many people had ever seen one up close. That all changed on September 21, 2012. On that day, the space shuttle *Endeavour* took its last flight. However, it didn't fly into space. It didn't fly to the moon or to another planet. It flew over the city of Los Angeles. It was strapped to a plane. The plane flew really low over the city. This was done so that the shuttle could be seen. Kids and adults looked up at the sky to watch it fly by.

When the plane landed, the shuttle was taken off. It was then put on a special vehicle that had many wheels. This was driven down the widest streets. It drove very slowly. It seemed to *crawl* along the street. This is because the shuttle was so heavy and big. It could not go fast!

The shuttle was taken to a museum. That museum is now the home of the shuttle. There is an exhibit there. This lets everyone visit the shuttle. Now, everyone can see *Endeavour* in its new home. Now you can really see it up close! You don't even have to look up at the sky.

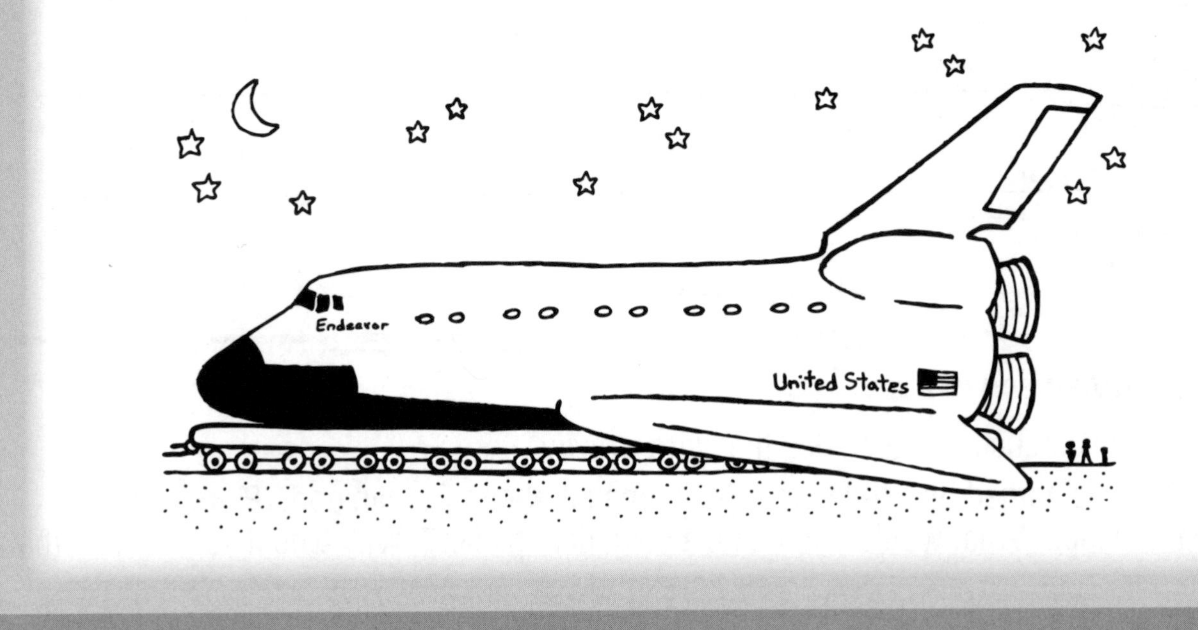

Name: ________________________

Answer the following questions about the story "A Home for *Endeavour*." The weights show you how hard you will need to work to find each answer.

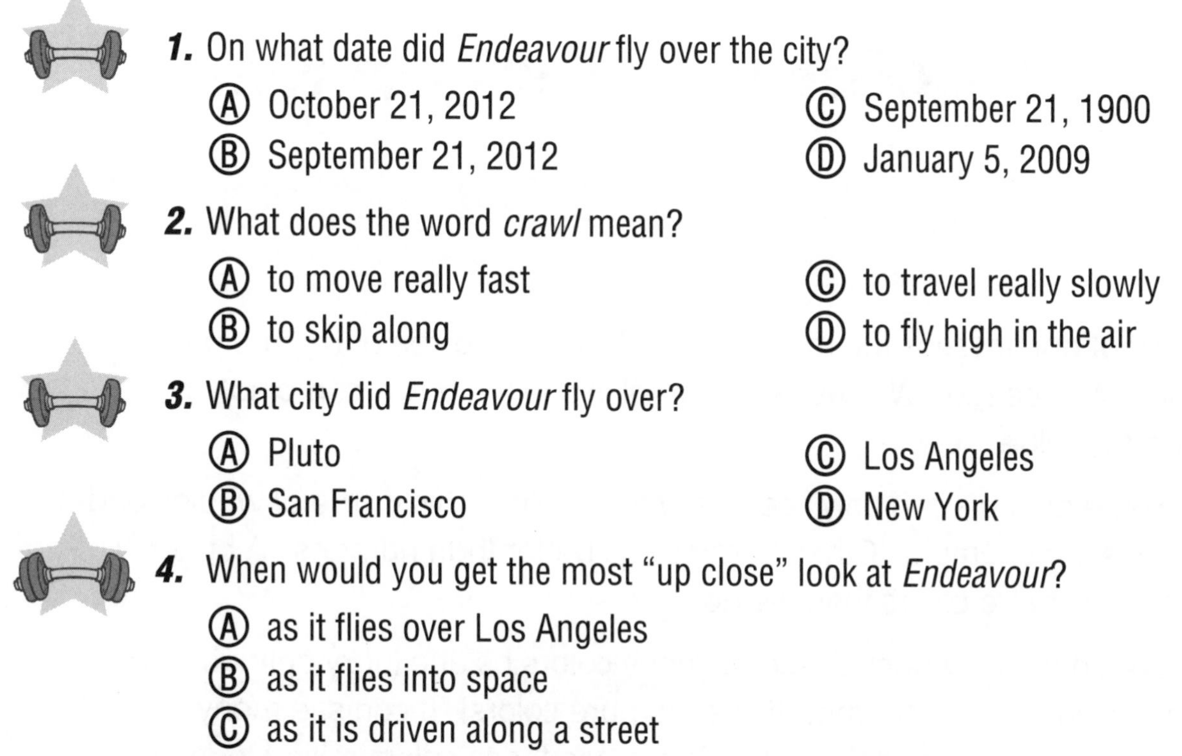

1. On what date did *Endeavour* fly over the city?

Ⓐ October 21, 2012
Ⓑ September 21, 2012
Ⓒ September 21, 1900
Ⓓ January 5, 2009

2. What does the word *crawl* mean?

Ⓐ to move really fast
Ⓑ to skip along
Ⓒ to travel really slowly
Ⓓ to fly high in the air

3. What city did *Endeavour* fly over?

Ⓐ Pluto
Ⓑ San Francisco
Ⓒ Los Angeles
Ⓓ New York

4. When would you get the most "up close" look at *Endeavour*?

Ⓐ as it flies over Los Angeles
Ⓑ as it flies into space
Ⓒ as it is driven along a street
Ⓓ at the museum exhibit

On the lines below, write your own question based on "A Home for *Endeavour*." Circle the correct picture on the left to show the level of the question you wrote.

On a separate piece of paper . . .

- Write a sentence that includes the word *exhibit*.
- Have you been to a museum before? What is something you have seen there?

Science Passage #5

The Colors a Shrimp Sees

What animal sees the most colors? Not us. We see only three pure colors. We see red. We see blue. We also see the many combinations of red and blue.

Some animals can only see one type of color. This is true of whales and dolphins, for example. Other animals see better than humans. A butterfly sees many more colors than we do.

Even a butterfly doesn't see as many colors as one lucky animal. That animal is the mantis shrimp. It sees 16 pure colors! It can see many combinations of those colors, too. It can see those colors mixed together. Try to imagine some of those fun, new colors! We cannot really do that. We cannot think about those colors and what they look like. We have never seen them.

The mantis shrimp lives in the ocean. Nobody knows why it *adapted* to see so many colors. When we say something has *adapted*, we mean that it has changed. This kind of change usually takes many years. Scientists think the shrimp changed in order to get food. The food it eats glows with colors. The mantis shrimp needed to see this food. It needed to be able to catch it. Seeing so many colors helps it eat. It must also make the shrimp's world very colorful!

Answer the following questions about the story "The Colors a Shrimp Sees." The weights show you how hard you will need to work to find each answer.

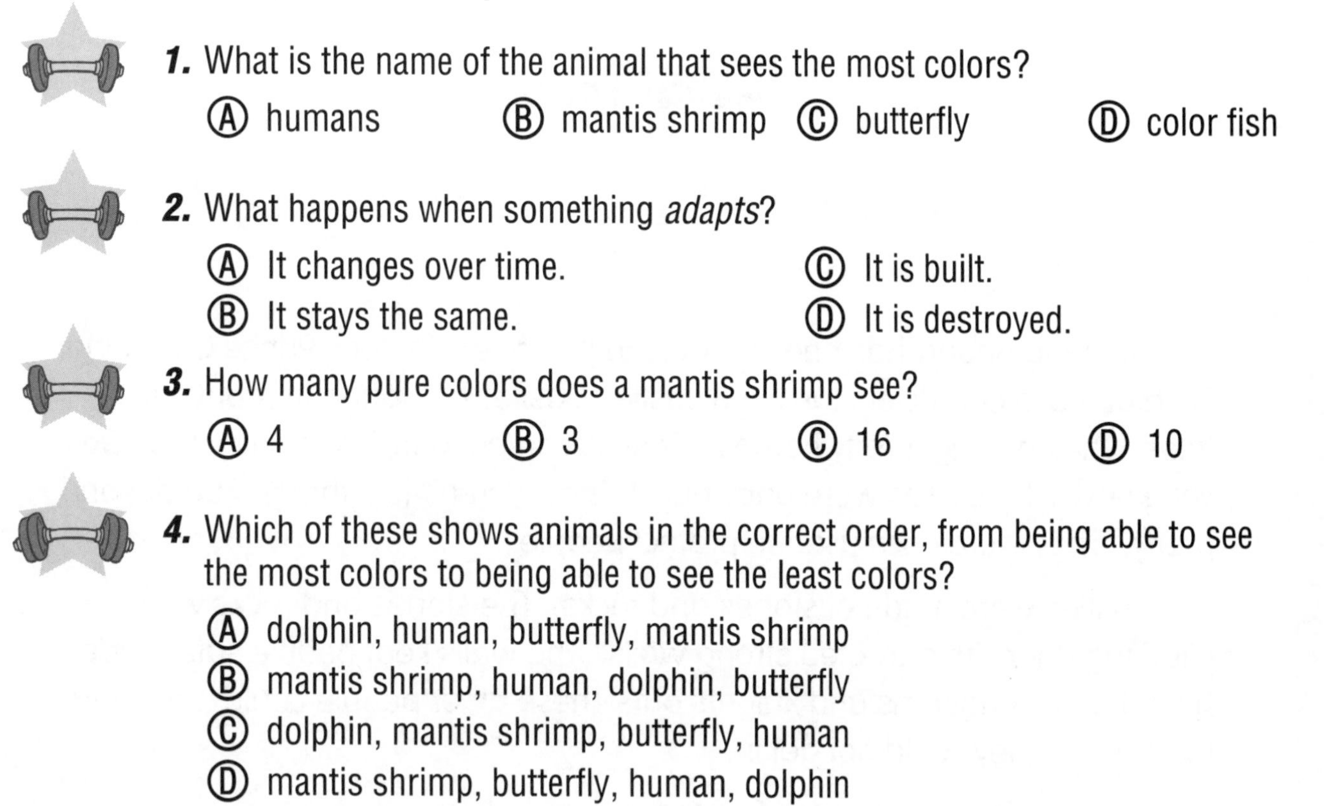

1. What is the name of the animal that sees the most colors?

Ⓐ humans Ⓑ mantis shrimp Ⓒ butterfly Ⓓ color fish

2. What happens when something *adapts*?

Ⓐ It changes over time.
Ⓑ It stays the same.
Ⓒ It is built.
Ⓓ It is destroyed.

3. How many pure colors does a mantis shrimp see?

Ⓐ 4 Ⓑ 3 Ⓒ 16 Ⓓ 10

4. Which of these shows animals in the correct order, from being able to see the most colors to being able to see the least colors?

Ⓐ dolphin, human, butterfly, mantis shrimp
Ⓑ mantis shrimp, human, dolphin, butterfly
Ⓒ dolphin, mantis shrimp, butterfly, human
Ⓓ mantis shrimp, butterfly, human, dolphin

On the lines below, write your own question based on "The Colors a Shrimp Sees." Circle the correct picture on the left to show the level of the question you wrote.

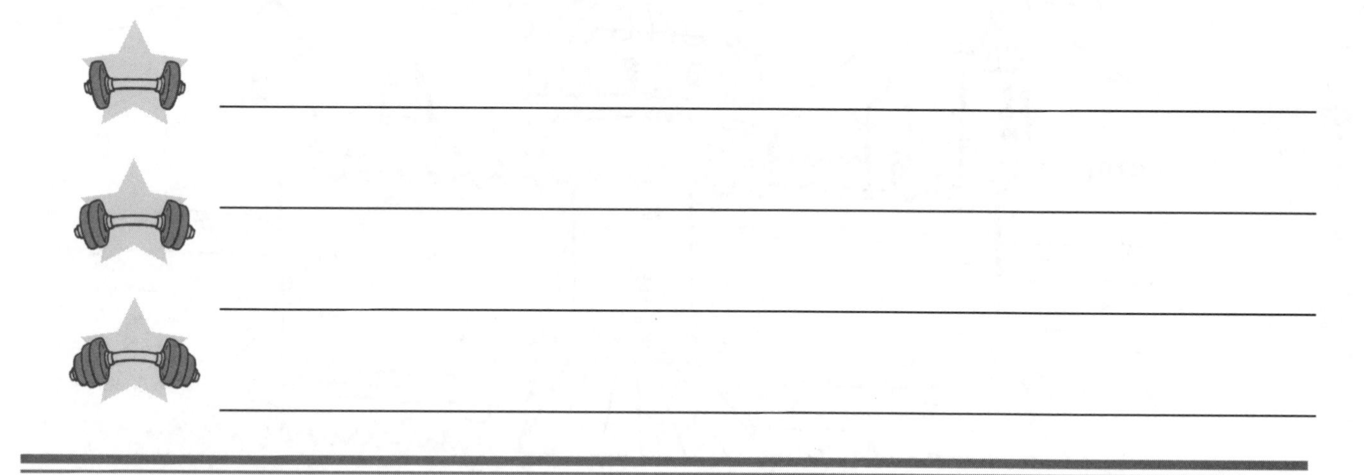

____

____

____

____

On a separate piece of paper . . .

- Write a sentence that includes the word *combinations*.
- Think about the colorful world of the mantis shrimp. Use crayons or markers to try to create a new color you've never seen before.

History
Passage
#1

Castles

Sleeping Beauty has one. Cinderella has one. So does Prince Charming. Each of these characters lives in a castle. Castles are found in many fairy tales. They are big, pretty homes. Castles can be found in real life, too. Do you know why castles were once built? They weren't just there to be big and pretty. They were once used to protect people.

Castles were made of stones and rocks. The stones and rocks were piled together. This created strong walls. The walls kept people safe inside. It kept other kingdoms and knights out. These other people could not *invade* the castle. They could not get in.

A castle has many parts. See the picture below:

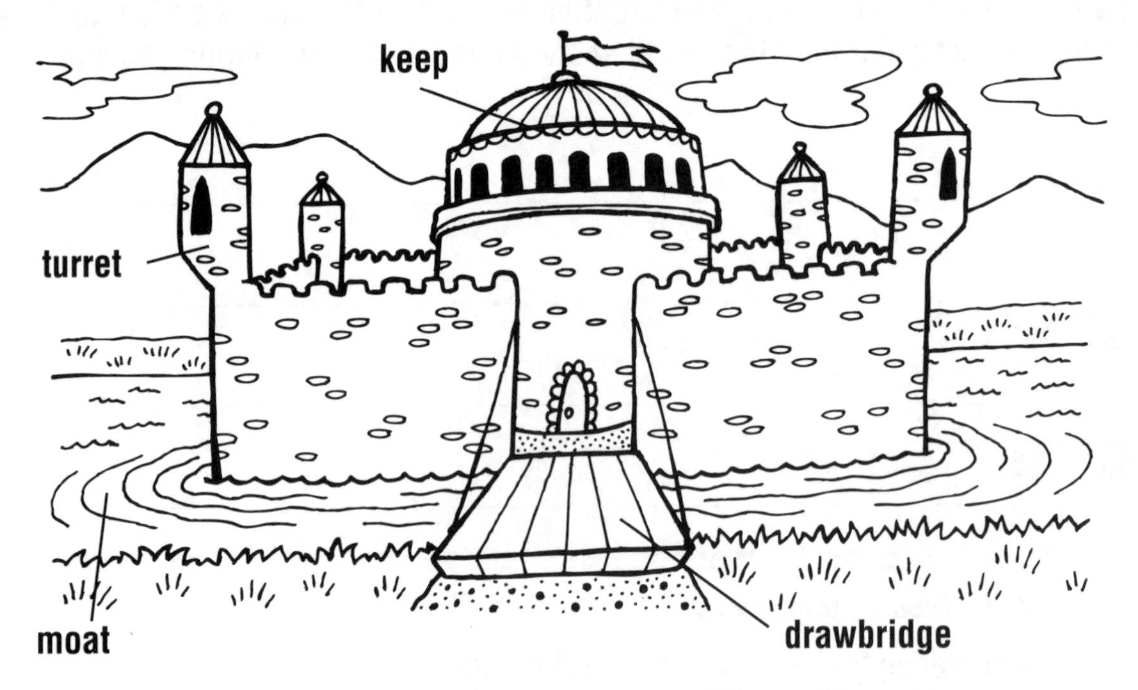

Castles are not built often today. You can still find old ones to see.

Answer the following questions about the story "Castles." The weights show you how hard you will need to work to find each answer.

1. The story says that castles were built long ago to

Ⓐ look pretty. Ⓒ store food.
Ⓑ protect people. Ⓓ invade others.

2. What does the story say was used to build the castles?

Ⓐ rocks and stones Ⓒ cement
Ⓑ sand and gravel Ⓓ wood

3. Based on the picture, what does the drawbridge do?

Ⓐ It is a diving board.
Ⓑ It is used for parades.
Ⓒ It can be lowered and raised to protect people.
Ⓓ It talks.

4. What does the word *invade* mean?

Ⓐ visit Ⓑ build Ⓒ cheer on Ⓓ attack

On the lines below, write your own question based on "Castles." Circle the correct picture on the left to show the level of the question you wrote.

____

____

____

____

On a separate piece of paper . . .

- Write a sentence that includes the word *characters*.
- Have you ever read about other castles? In what other stories do castles appear? Create a list of how many you remember.

History Passage #2

How They Got Their Name

Most kids know what a Lego® is. Kids have been playing with these popular toys for years. Most legos are plastic cubes. These cubes have little pegs on the top. They have little holes on the bottom. The little pegs on the top fit into the little holes on the bottom. A child can stack the cubes. He or she can also pull them apart again. These cubes were invented in the 1930s. They were invented in Denmark. That is when they were named. Do you know how they got their name?

To name the new toy, the inventor had a contest. Someone came up with the name *leg godt*. This means "play well." Soon the name became "Lego." The inventor found out that the word "lego" also meant something else. In Latin, the word *lego* means "I put together."

For years, kids have been using Legos. They have been putting them together and playing well. What a fitting name for a great toy!

Answer the following questions about the story "How They Got Their Name." The weights show you how hard you will need to work to find each answer.

1. Where were Legos invented?

Ⓐ Denmark
Ⓑ San Diego
Ⓒ Detroit
Ⓓ Delaware

2. According to the passage, what shape are most Legos?

Ⓐ spheres
Ⓑ pyramids
Ⓒ cubes
Ⓓ cylinders

3. What does *leg godt* mean?

Ⓐ "can't play"
Ⓑ "play well"
Ⓒ "play with cards"
Ⓓ "won't play with others"

4. What does the word *fitting* mean in "What a fitting name for a great toy!"?

Ⓐ The name fits inside another name.
Ⓑ The name is a great toy.
Ⓒ The name is from Denmark.
Ⓓ The name is a perfect name for the toy.

On the lines below, write your own question based on "How They Got Their Name." Circle the correct picture on the left to show the level of the question you wrote.

On a separate piece of paper . . .

- Write a sentence that includes the word *inventor.*
- Have you ever wanted to invent something? Draw a picture of a new kind of toy.

History Passage #3

Big Dinosaur, Small Brain

The Stegosaurus was a dinosaur. It lived a long time ago. It lived millions of years ago. Stegosaurus means "plated lizard." It ate plants. It is known for its long row of spikes. These big spikes might have helped to keep its temperature just right.

The Stegosaurus was big. It was about 25 feet long. That's about as large as a bus. It's also about as long as you and four of your friends. If all five of you laid feet to head, you would be about as long as the Stegosaurus.

So this animal was huge. It probably was not very smart, though. Scientists suspect that it wasn't smart because its brain was so small. They suspect it, but they are not sure.

How small was this creature's brain? It was only the size of a walnut! Just imagine a bus with a walnut on its hood! There you have the *mighty* Stegosaurus!

Answer the following questions about the story "Big Dinosaur, Small Brain." The weights show you how hard you will need to work to find each answer.

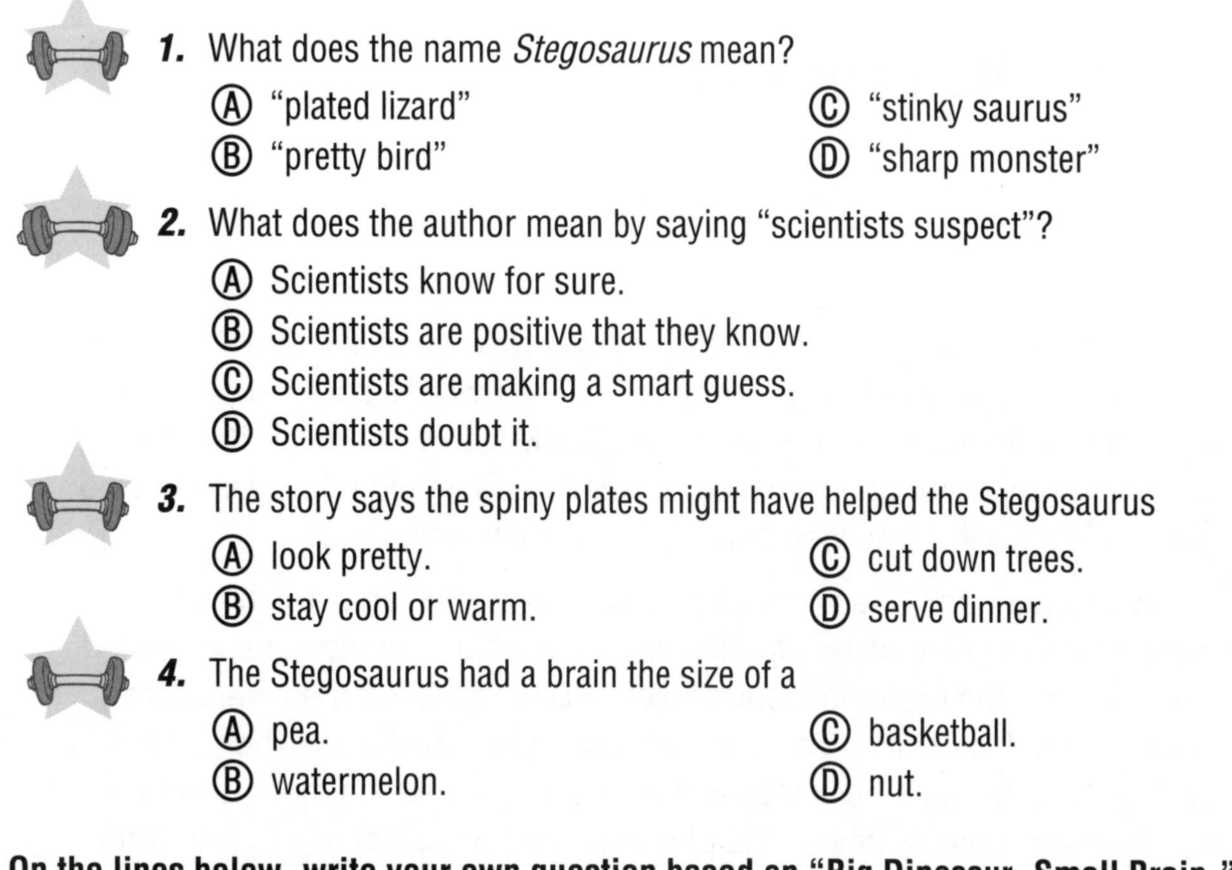

1. What does the name *Stegosaurus* mean?

Ⓐ "plated lizard"
Ⓑ "pretty bird"
Ⓒ "stinky saurus"
Ⓓ "sharp monster"

2. What does the author mean by saying "scientists suspect"?

Ⓐ Scientists know for sure.
Ⓑ Scientists are positive that they know.
Ⓒ Scientists are making a smart guess.
Ⓓ Scientists doubt it.

3. The story says the spiny plates might have helped the Stegosaurus

Ⓐ look pretty.
Ⓑ stay cool or warm.
Ⓒ cut down trees.
Ⓓ serve dinner.

4. The Stegosaurus had a brain the size of a

Ⓐ pea.
Ⓑ watermelon.
Ⓒ basketball.
Ⓓ nut.

On the lines below, write your own question based on "Big Dinosaur, Small Brain." Circle the correct picture on the left to show the level of the question you wrote.

____

____

____

____

On a separate piece of paper . . .

- Write a sentence that includes the word *mighty*.
- The passage says that the dinosaur was the size of a bus with a brain the size of a walnut. Draw the bus with a walnut on its hood.

History Passage #4

The History of the Fire Truck

It is really exciting to see fire trucks. They race down the street. They are on their way to save buildings. They are on their way to save people. Years ago, this would not have happened. Fire trucks could not race! They started as water pumps that people pulled. Sometimes it would take a long time to get to a fire. By the time they arrived, the firemen were tired!

What changed? The water pumps were *mounted* on something that moved. They were attached to the top of a moving platform. Horses pulled the platform. The men ran alongside of it. Even then, the men were tired when they got to the fire. Then, somebody had a good idea. They added running boards and a back step to the wagon. This let the men ride to the fire. But with more weight on the platform, the horses got more tired. They traveled slower and slower.

Then, in the 1840s, the steam engine helped. Think of fire trucks as steam trains racing down the street. They were strong but not really safe. Finally, in the 1900s, fire trucks became motorized like the trucks of today.

Name: ______________________________ History Passage #4

Answer the following questions about the story "The History of the Fire Truck." The weights show you how hard you will need to work to find each answer.

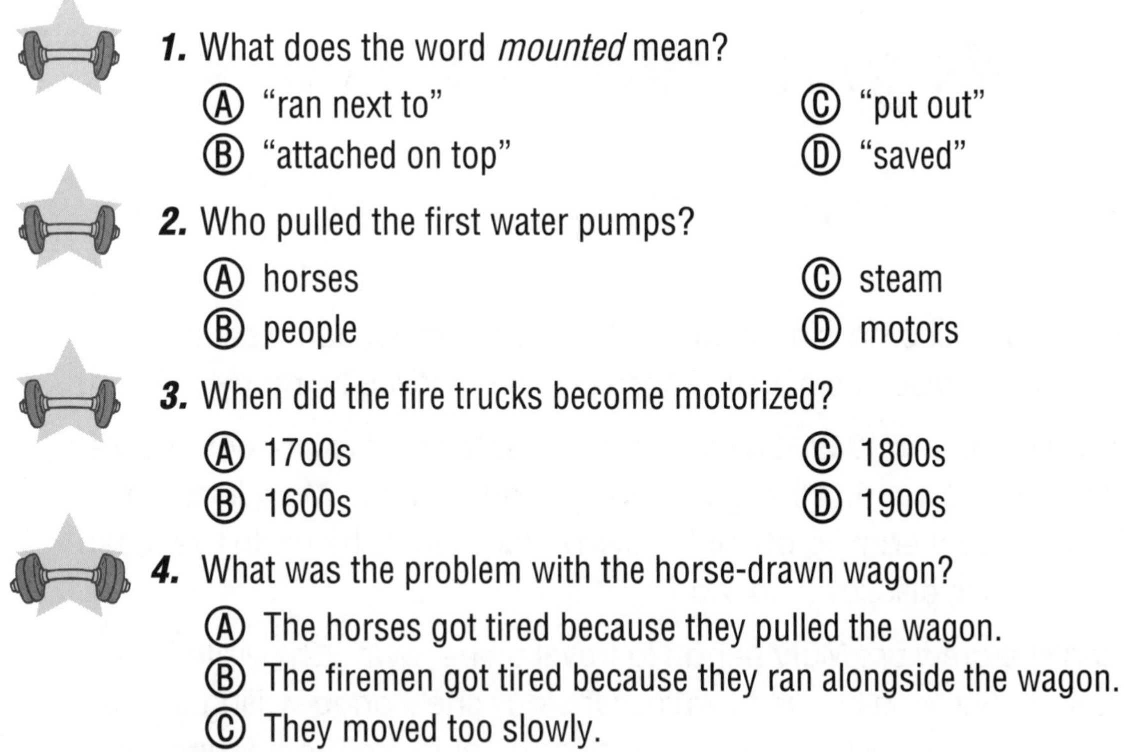

1. What does the word *mounted* mean?

Ⓐ "ran next to" Ⓒ "put out"
Ⓑ "attached on top" Ⓓ "saved"

2. Who pulled the first water pumps?

Ⓐ horses Ⓒ steam
Ⓑ people Ⓓ motors

3. When did the fire trucks become motorized?

Ⓐ 1700s Ⓒ 1800s
Ⓑ 1600s Ⓓ 1900s

4. What was the problem with the horse-drawn wagon?

Ⓐ The horses got tired because they pulled the wagon.
Ⓑ The firemen got tired because they ran alongside the wagon.
Ⓒ They moved too slowly.
Ⓓ All of the above.

On the lines below, write your own question based on "The History of the Fire Truck." Circle the correct picture on the left to show the level of the question you wrote.

On a separate piece of paper . . .

- Write a sentence that includes the word *arrived.*
- Think about the fire trucks of today. How can they be improved? Think of a way to make fire trucks better. Draw a picture of your new truck.

Biographical Passage #1

A Magical Way to Travel

Mary Pope Osborne is a famous author. She has written a series of books about a magic tree house. These books are loved by many children.

Mary was born in 1949. Her father was a soldier. This job took Mary's family all over the world. Mary got to live in many places. Mary loved to travel. She loved dreaming about far-away places that she hadn't yet been to. In school, she also loved to read.

When she grew up, Mary began to travel on her own. She visited even more places. She also began to write. One day she started writing about two children named Jack and Annie. Jack and Annie are brother and sister. They find a magic tree house. This tree house takes them to far-away lands. It also lets them travel to other times.

The *Magic Tree House* series became very popular. Mary kept writing them. Now there are about 50 books in the series. Through these books, Mary shares her love of traveling. She shows children all over the world how much there is to see and how many adventures they can have.

Answer the following questions about the story "A Magical Way to Travel." The weights show you how hard you will need to work to find each answer.

1. About how many *Magic Tree House* books has Mary Pope Osborne written?

Ⓐ 31 Ⓒ 22
Ⓑ 50 Ⓓ 15

2. From the story, what can you tell is true about any series of books?

Ⓐ They are always about magic.
Ⓑ They are always very popular.
Ⓒ They are always written about children.
Ⓓ There are always made up of more than one book.

3. What inspired Mary to write?

Ⓐ her travels Ⓒ the military
Ⓑ her father Ⓓ tree houses

4. What are the names of the main characters in the *Magic Tree House* books?

Ⓐ Jack and Diane Ⓒ Mary and Osborne
Ⓑ Annie and John Ⓓ Jack and Annie

On the lines below, write your own question based on "A Magical Way to Travel." Circle the correct picture on the left to show the level of the question you wrote.

____

____

____

____

On a separate piece of paper . . .

- Write a sentence that includes the word *adventures*.
- Where do you think Jack and Annie should go in the next *Magic Tree House* book? Why?

Biographical Passage #2

The Man Who Did So Much

Benjamin Franklin is a famous American. He lived long ago, and he did many things. He helped make laws. He wrote books. He was a great leader. He even started the U.S. Post Office. He must have been busy! That didn't stop him from also being a great inventor.

Here is a list of just some of his inventions or discoveries:

1. **Swim Fins** — He made flippers to swim with. They were worn on your hands, not your feet. Ben invented these when he was just 11 years old!
2. **Electricity** — Ben studied electricity. He helped people understand what it was all about.
3. **The Gulf Stream** — The Gulf Stream is like a fast-moving road in the ocean. It makes ships move faster or slower. Ben studied this strong *current*. Then, he mapped it.
4. **"Long Arm"** — Have you ever wanted something that was hard to reach? Ben made a long stick with a grasping end. That way he could reach for things high up.

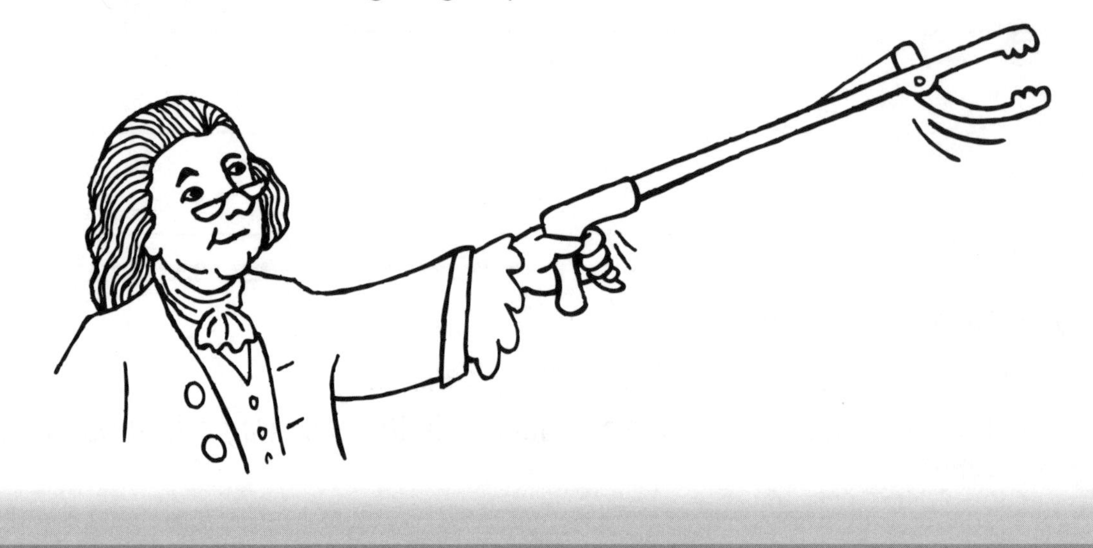

Answer the following questions about the story "The Man Who Did So Much." The weights show you how hard you will need to work to find each answer.

1. Look at the title of the passage. What does the author think of Benjamin Franklin?

Ⓐ that he was lazy
Ⓑ that he was a good cook
Ⓒ that he did a lot of different things
Ⓓ that he was a good fireman

2. What did Benjamin Franklin create?

Ⓐ paper
Ⓑ television
Ⓒ the U.S. Post Office
Ⓓ pencils

3. In the way it is used in the story, what does the word *current* mean?

Ⓐ a path of fast-moving water
Ⓑ a bolt of eletricity
Ⓒ a piece of fruit
Ⓓ something that is happening now

4. What piece of clothing were Benjamin Franklin's swim fins most like?

Ⓐ pants Ⓑ belt Ⓒ shoes Ⓓ gloves

On the lines below, write your own question based on "The Man Who Did So Much." Circle the correct picture on the left to show the level of the question you wrote.

On a separate piece of paper . . .

- Write a sentence that includes the word *invention.*
- Think of a new invention that nobody has ever thought of before! Describe it.

Biographical Passage #3

The "Fab Four" Friends

The place was London. The year was 1957. A young high school student dreamed of making music. The boy's name was John Lennon. He started a rock band. He got another friend of his to join his new group. The other boy's name was Paul McCartney. Then, a younger student, George Harrison, joined the band. John, Paul, and George all played guitar. They needed the right drummer. Five years later, they found one. His name was Ringo Starr.

Together, the four friends became one of the greatest music groups of all time. The band's name was The Beatles. These four friends became known as the Fab Four. Until 1970, they toured around the world, singing and bringing new music to the people. Twenty of their songs became #1 hits. Their music is still listened to and loved today. In all, the Beatles have sold about one billion records. No band has sold more.

Answer the following questions about the story "The 'Fab Four' Friends." The weights show you how hard you will need to work to find each answer.

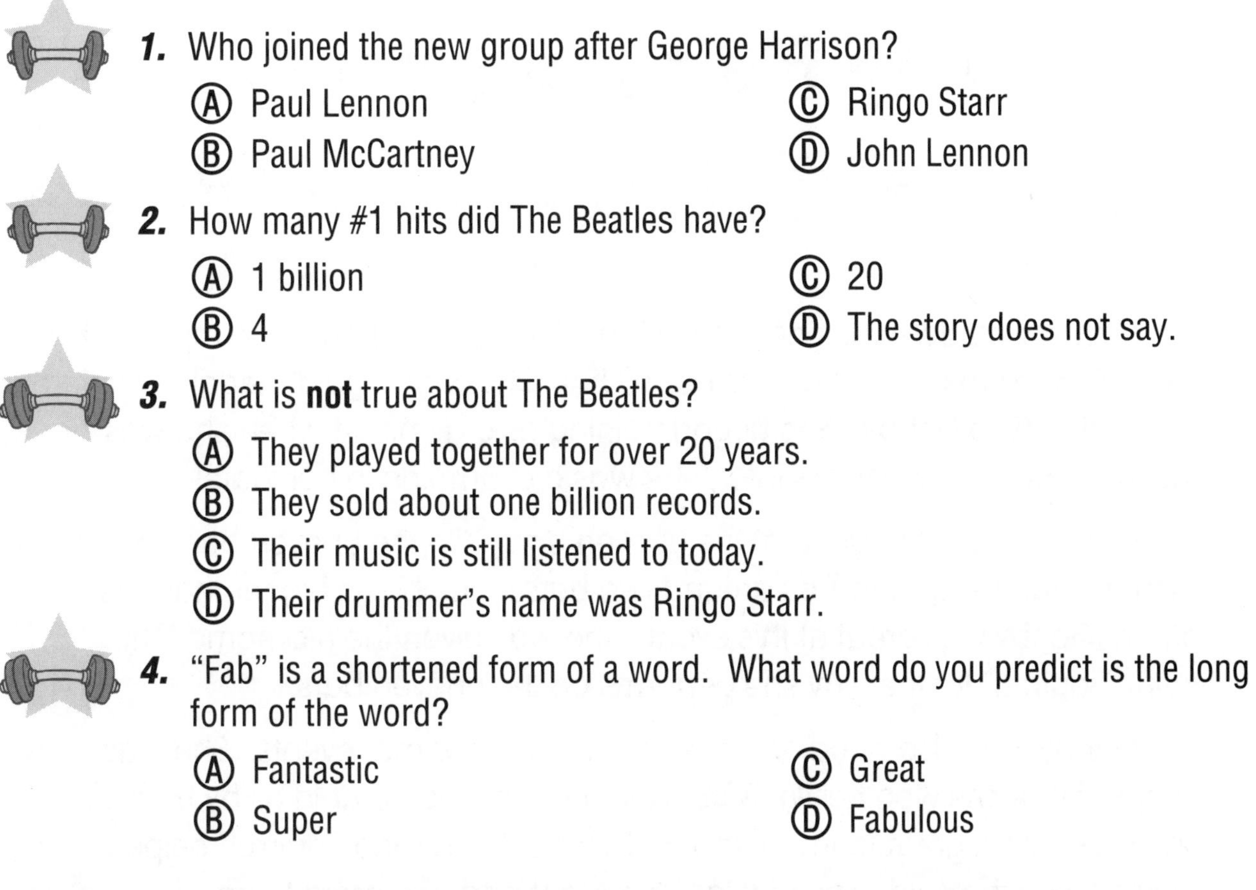

1. Who joined the new group after George Harrison?

Ⓐ Paul Lennon
Ⓑ Paul McCartney
Ⓒ Ringo Starr
Ⓓ John Lennon

2. How many #1 hits did The Beatles have?

Ⓐ 1 billion
Ⓑ 4
Ⓒ 20
Ⓓ The story does not say.

3. What is **not** true about The Beatles?

Ⓐ They played together for over 20 years.
Ⓑ They sold about one billion records.
Ⓒ Their music is still listened to today.
Ⓓ Their drummer's name was Ringo Starr.

4. "Fab" is a shortened form of a word. What word do you predict is the long form of the word?

Ⓐ Fantastic
Ⓑ Super
Ⓒ Great
Ⓓ Fabulous

On the lines below, write your own question based on "The 'Fab Four' Friends." Circle the correct picture on the left to show the level of the question you wrote.

On a separate piece of paper . . .

- Write a sentence that includes the word *joined.*
- If you could play any musical instrument, what would it be? Why?

Biographical Passage #4

The Flying Squirrel

Gabby Douglas was one of the stars of the 2012 Summer Olympics. She was 17. She was a gymnast for Team USA. She won a gold medal. Winning was not new to Gabby. She began training as a gymnast when she was just 6 years old. Two years later, she was a champion in her state!

Gabby was really good at the uneven bars. On the uneven bars, a gymnast jumps up and flips around two bars. One bar is higher than the other. Gabby was great at this event. She was given the nickname "The Flying Squirrel" for the way she performs on the uneven bars.

Gabby was also good at the vault and the floor mat events. She was so good that she won her *individual* events. She won a gold all by herself. She was also a great team member. In 2012 "The Flying Squirrel" helped the USA win the gold. She was an important part of a great team.

Answer the following questions about the story "The Flying Squirrel." The weights show you how hard you will need to work to find each answer.

1. Why might Gabby Douglas be called "The Flying Squirrel"?

Ⓐ She runs really fast.
Ⓑ She is a great swimmer.
Ⓒ She is a great gymnast.
Ⓓ She likes squirrels.

2. How old was Gabby Douglas when she began training?

Ⓐ 14
Ⓑ 8
Ⓒ 6
Ⓓ 17

3. What does the word *individual* mean?

Ⓐ with a group
Ⓑ with a partner
Ⓒ as a team
Ⓓ all by one's self

4. Why did the author put an exclamation point at the end of the first paragraph?

Ⓐ to show amazement
Ⓑ to show confusion
Ⓒ to show anger
Ⓓ to show boredom

On the lines below, write your own question based on "The Flying Squirrel." Circle the correct picture on the left to show the level of the question you wrote.

On a separate piece of paper . . .

- Write a sentence that includes the word *training*.
- If you could train for any event in the Olympics, which would you choose? Why?

Informational Passage #1

Some More, Please!

Have you ever eaten a s'more? A s'more is a delicious treat. It was first created by a Girl Scout many years ago.

A s'more is like a little sandwich. Its filling is made by combining chocolate and marshmallow. Want to learn exactly how to make a s'more? Here's how!

1. Take one graham cracker.
2. Have a grown-up roast a marshmallow on a stick over a fire.
3. Put a square of chocolate on the cracker.
4. Put the marshmallow on the chocolate.
5. Put another piece of cracker on the marshmallow like a sandwich.
6. Enjoy!

A s'more is a tasty treat with an unusual name. How did it get its name? The word *s'more* is made by combining two words. It is made by putting together the words *some* and *more*. Mash those two words together, and you get *s'more*! You do this just like you mash together chocolate and marshmallow to make a s'more's filling. Once you taste a s'more, you might know why it is has this name. You will probably want some more!

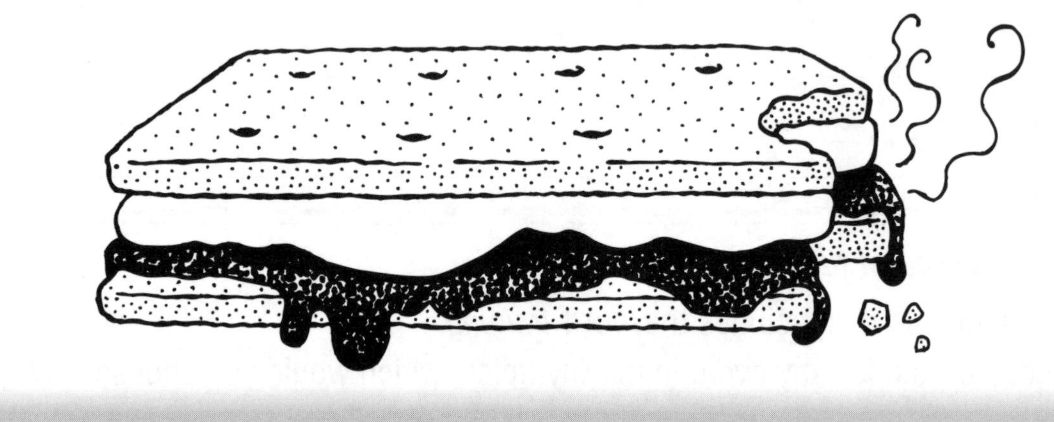

Answer the following questions about the story "Some More, Please!" The weights show you how hard you will need to work to find each answer.

1. What does the word *roast* mean?

Ⓐ cook
Ⓑ open
Ⓒ chop up
Ⓓ spread

2. What tool do you use to roast the marshmallow?

Ⓐ fork
Ⓑ knife
Ⓒ campfire
Ⓓ stick

3. What is combined to make the word *s'more*?

Ⓐ chocolate and marshmallow
Ⓑ graham crackers, chocolate, and marshmallow
Ⓒ the words *some* and *more*
Ⓓ fire and a stick

4. The author says a s'more is like a sandwich. Which part of a s'more is like the bread on a sandwich?

Ⓐ stick
Ⓑ chocolate
Ⓒ marshmallow
Ⓓ graham cracker

On the lines below, write your own question based on "Some More, Please!" Circle the correct picture on the left to show the level of the question you wrote.

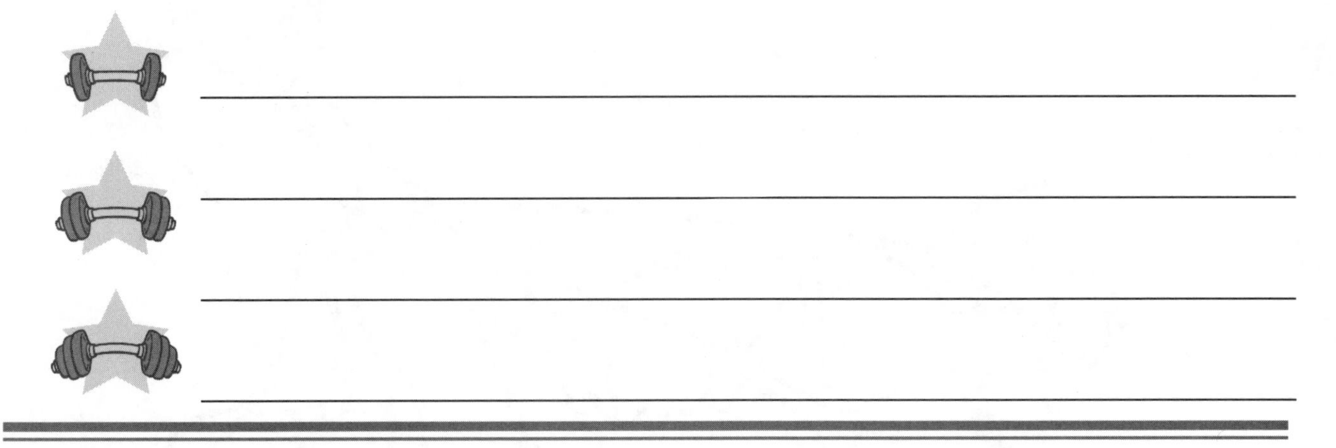

On a separate piece of paper . . .

- Write a sentence that includes the word *combining*.
- Can you make up a word that combines two other words together?

Informational Passage #2

Taking Care of a Dog

Owning a dog takes a lot of work. You have to feed it. You have to give it water. You have to let it outside to go to the bathroom. You have to walk it to give it exercise. You also have to train it so everyone is happy being around the dog. What can you train a dog to do?

You can train a dog how to do simple things like. . .

1. sit down
2. come when it is called
3. stay on a mark when you walk away

All of these points are important to do when taking care of a dog. However, the most important thing to remember is to love it.

Answer the following questions about the story "Taking Care of a Dog." The weights show you how hard you will need to work to find each answer.

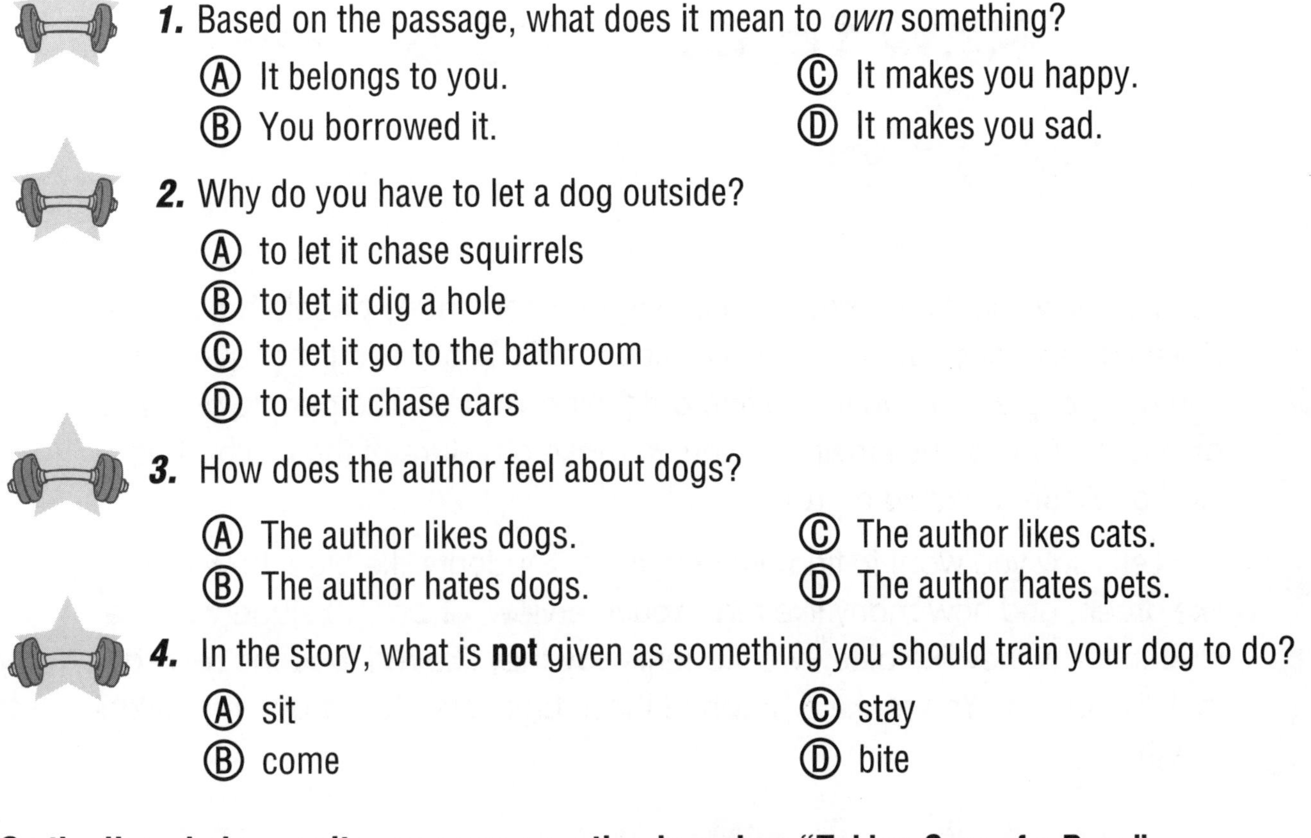

1. Based on the passage, what does it mean to *own* something?

Ⓐ It belongs to you.
Ⓑ You borrowed it.
Ⓒ It makes you happy.
Ⓓ It makes you sad.

2. Why do you have to let a dog outside?

Ⓐ to let it chase squirrels
Ⓑ to let it dig a hole
Ⓒ to let it go to the bathroom
Ⓓ to let it chase cars

3. How does the author feel about dogs?

Ⓐ The author likes dogs.
Ⓑ The author hates dogs.
Ⓒ The author likes cats.
Ⓓ The author hates pets.

4. In the story, what is **not** given as something you should train your dog to do?

Ⓐ sit
Ⓑ come
Ⓒ stay
Ⓓ bite

On the lines below, write your own question based on "Taking Care of a Dog." Circle the correct picture on the left to show the level of the question you wrote.

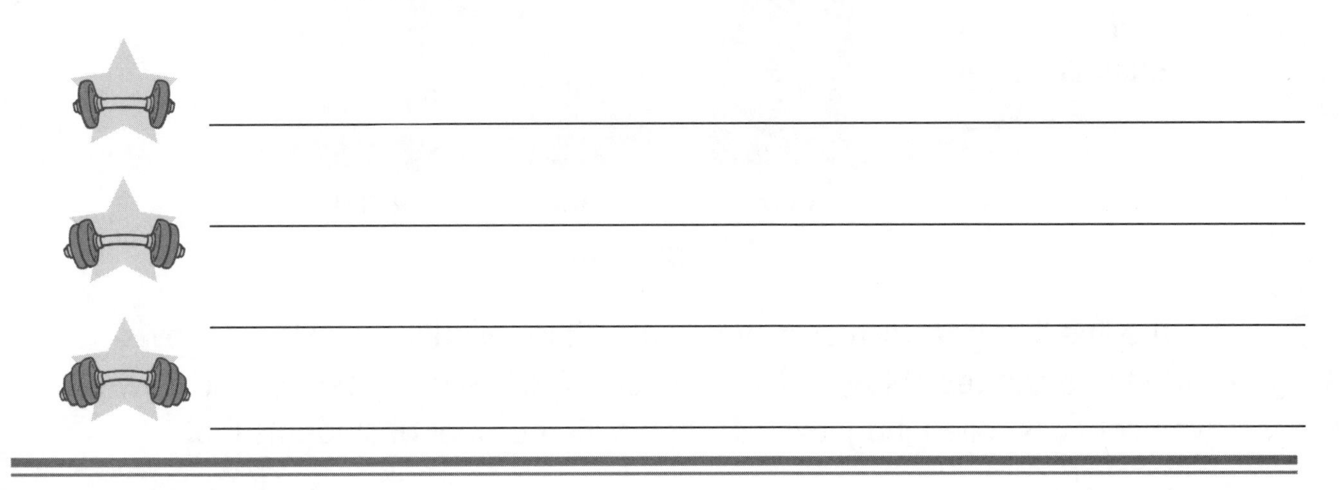

On a separate piece of paper . . .

- Write a sentence that includes the word *exercise.*
- Do you own a pet? Write a sentence about what kind of pet you have or want to have.

Informational Passage #3

How to Create a Poll

Let's say you are interested in finding out how many people have a pet. It would be easy to do this if you created a poll. A poll is a list of questions you ask people. You do this to find out their opinions. The people give you answers. You can use their answers to make a picture of the math. This kind of picture is called a graph.

Let's say you want to find out how many students like blue, how many like green, and how many like red. You interview, or ask, 10 students. Five students say they like blue, two students say they like red, and the rest say they like green. You make a graph of these answers. The graph might look like this:

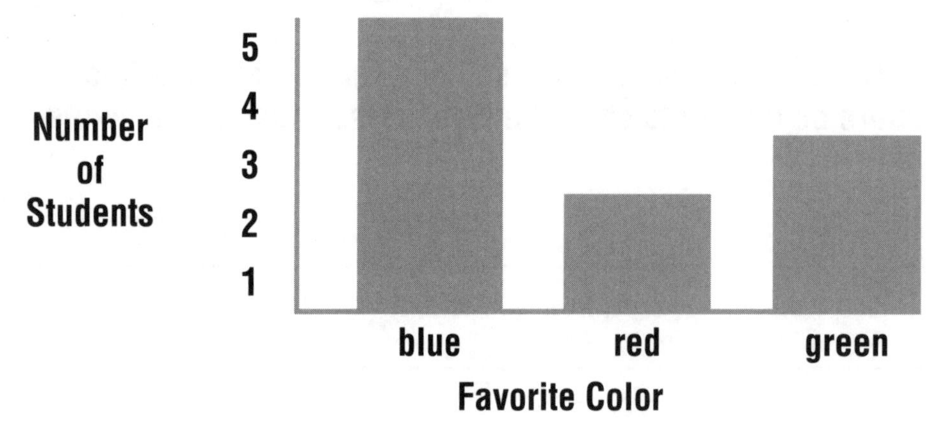

The line that goes across is horizontal. It is called the *x*-axis. It shows us the three choices: blue, red, and green. The line that goes up and down is vertical. It is called the *y*-axis. It shows the number of students that were polled.

So the next time you need to find out how people feel about a problem, you can use a poll. First, come up with a question. Then, interview a group of people. Then, create a graph so you can see a picture of the numbers.

Answer the following questions about the story "How to Create a Poll." The weights show you how hard you will need to work to find each answer.

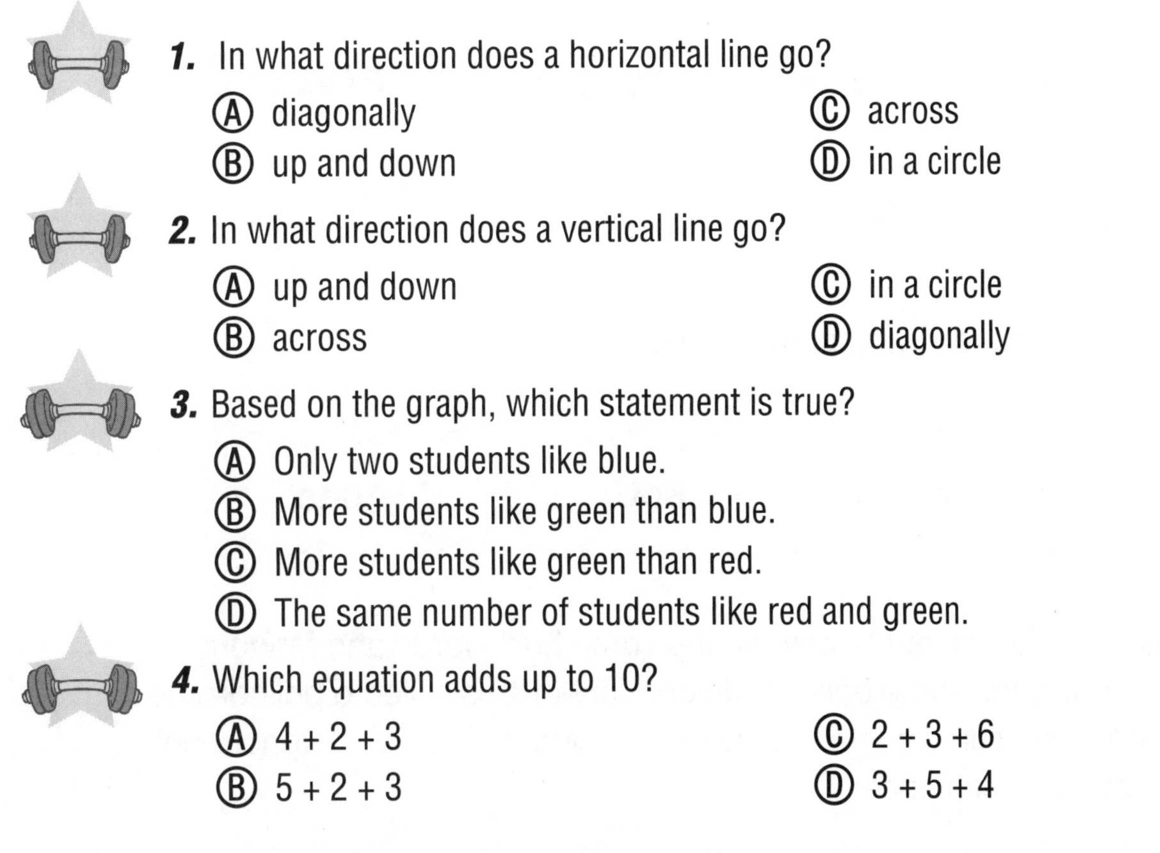

1. In what direction does a horizontal line go?
   - Ⓐ diagonally
   - Ⓑ up and down
   - Ⓒ across
   - Ⓓ in a circle

2. In what direction does a vertical line go?
   - Ⓐ up and down
   - Ⓑ across
   - Ⓒ in a circle
   - Ⓓ diagonally

3. Based on the graph, which statement is true?
   - Ⓐ Only two students like blue.
   - Ⓑ More students like green than blue.
   - Ⓒ More students like green than red.
   - Ⓓ The same number of students like red and green.

4. Which equation adds up to 10?
   - Ⓐ $4 + 2 + 3$
   - Ⓑ $5 + 2 + 3$
   - Ⓒ $2 + 3 + 6$
   - Ⓓ $3 + 5 + 4$

On the lines below, write your own question based on "How to Create a Poll." Circle the correct picture on the left to show the level of the question you wrote.

____

____

____

____

On a separate piece of paper . . .

- Write a sentence that includes the word *interview*.
- Interview five people about their favorite color. Then, show your answer by drawing a graph of the results.

Informational Passage #4

What Is a Palindrome?

What do the following names have in common?

Did you figure it out? They are the same backwards and forwards! A word that is the same backwards and forwards is called a palindrome. There are even some sentences that are palindromes. For instance, look at the following sentence:

Was it a car or a cat I saw?

Now look at each letter. Look from the first letter to the last. Look at the "W" in *Was* and the "w" in *saw*. They are the same letter. Then look at the second letter in the sentence and the second-to-last letter. They are the same, too! Keep doing this. You will see it is the same letter each time. The sentence is the same in both directions!

Look around you. Can you think of any other words or sentences that are palindromes? There are more around than you might think. Maybe even the name of a student right next to you is a palindrome!

Answer the following questions about the story "What Is a Palindrome?" The weights show you how hard you will need to work to find each answer.

1. Which name is **not** a palindrome?

Ⓐ Bob
Ⓑ Otto
Ⓒ Mimi
Ⓓ Ana

2. Which date is a palindrome?

Ⓐ 1900
Ⓑ 2002
Ⓒ 2012
Ⓓ 2020

3. What is the last letter needed to make the following sentence into a palindrome?

"Madam, I'm Ada_"

Ⓐ d
Ⓑ a
Ⓒ i
Ⓓ m

4. If you wrote the phrase "Ma has a ham" *backwards*, what would it be?

Ⓐ Ma has a ham
Ⓑ Ham is good
Ⓒ Ma has a pig
Ⓓ Ham is for mom

On the lines below, write your own question based on "What Is a Palindrome?" Circle the correct picture on the left to show the level of the question you wrote.

____

____

____

____

On a separate piece of paper . . .

- Write a sentence that includes the word *forwards*.
- Can you think of any palindromes? Use one that you have heard before or try to make one up that nobody knows about yet!

Making Paper Fly

Making a paper airplane is pretty simple if you practice. It only takes six steps:

Step 1: Get a regular piece of paper. It should be a rectangle, not a square.

Step 2: Fold the paper in half. We call this fold a "hot dog" fold because it makes the paper look like a long rectangle. Unfold it so you see the folded line going down the center of the paper.

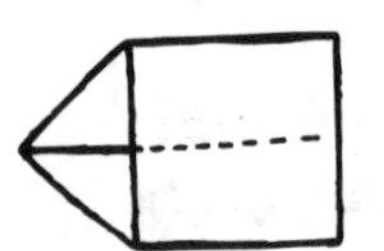

Step 3: Take the two corners at the top and fold them towards the folded line. This will make a point at the top like the point of a triangle.

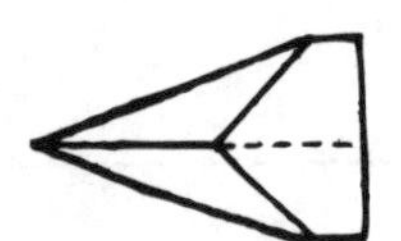

Step 4: Fold the sides in towards the center line again. This time, the triangle point will become more narrow.

Step 5: Fold the middle of the paper in half. It should now look like you are looking at the side of an airplane.

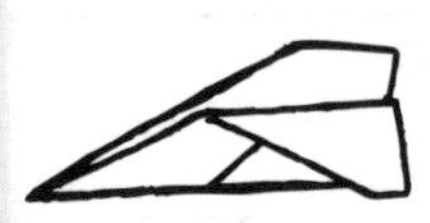

Step 6: Fold each side down so it meets the bottom of the plane.

Decorate and fly! Your plane should now be ready to go!

Answer the following questions about the story "Making Paper Fly." The weights show you how hard you will need to work to find each answer.

1. How many steps does it take to make a simple paper airplane?

Ⓐ 1
Ⓑ 3
Ⓒ 5
Ⓓ 6

2. What kind of fold is recommended?

Ⓐ "hamburger" fold
Ⓑ "triangle" fold
Ⓒ "hot dog" fold
Ⓓ "pizza" fold

3. What shape of paper should you begin with?

Ⓐ triangle
Ⓑ square
Ⓒ circle
Ⓓ rectangle

4. If the story had said there are seven steps to making a paper airplane, what would it have said is the seventh step?

Ⓐ Buy a piece of paper.
Ⓑ Decorate your airplane.
Ⓒ Cut your paper into a square shape.
Ⓓ Eat a hot dog.

On the lines below, write your own question based on "Making Paper Fly." Circle the correct picture on the left to show the level of the question you wrote.

On a separate piece of paper . . .

- Write a sentence that includes the word *fold*.
- Reading the directions above, make the paper airplane. Describe how it flies.

Answer Key

Accept appropriate responses for the final three entries on the question-and-answer pages.

The Star of the Sea (page 11)
1. B
2. A
3. D
4. D

Matter Matters (page 13)
1. C
2. A
3. D
4. B

The Fish with the Big Mouth (page 15)
1. B
2. B
3. D
4. D

Not a Planet Now (page 17)
1. C
2. B
3. B
4. D

A Home for *Endeavour* (page 19)
1. B
2. C
3. C
4. D

The Colors a Shrimp Sees (page 21)
1. B
2. A
3. C
4. D

Castles (page 23)
1. B
2. A
3. C
4. D

How They Got Their Name (page 25)
1. A
2. C
3. B
4. D

Big Dinosaur, Small Brain (page 27)
1. A
2. C
3. B
4. D

The History of the Fire Truck (page 29)
1. B
2. B
3. D
4. D

A Magical Way to Travel (page 31)
1. B
2. D
3. A
4. D

The Man Who Did So Much (page 33)
1. C
2. C
3. A
4. D

The "Fab Four" Friends (page 35)
1. C
2. C
3. A
4. D

The Flying Squirrel (page 37)
1. C
2. C
3. D
4. A

Some More, Please! (page 39)
1. A
2. D
3. C
4. D

Taking Care of a Dog (page 41)
1. A
2. C
3. A
4. D

How to Create a Poll (page 43)
1. C
2. A
3. C
4. B

What Is a Palindrome? (page 45)
1. C
2. B
3. D
4. A

Making Paper Fly (page 47)
1. D
2. C
3. D
4. B